Debugging Your Brain

Casey Watts!

First Printing, 2020

ISBN 978-0-578-75503-8

https://caseywatts.com

This book was written, illustrated, typeset, and published by Casey Watts.

https://caseywatts.com

Thank you Jiaqi Dai for creating the beautiful cover art.

http://www.jiaqidai.me

Thank you everyone who reviewed early copies of the book, and to everyone who provided encouragement along the way.

The human brain is buggy. Sometimes your mind distorts reality, gets stuck on shortcomings, or spirals out of control. With the right tools, you can patch the software that runs in your mind: catch distortions of reality, transform frustration into insight, and short-circuit downward spirals. Become a better friend, team member, and human.

The brain is a complex system. Debugging Your Brain is a toolkit to help you understand and optimize yours.

"A straightforward and easily digestible read that decodes several basic, but complex concepts in psychology. With a little practice, the topics and techniques covered in this book will help train your brain how to deal with any situation effectively and productively. The author's lighthearted and relatable way of writing makes it an enjoyable read."

— Dr. Melissa Monsey
Neuroscience Ph.D.
Yale University

"Casey has a gift to make very complex information in a manner that everyone can understand and apply."

— Joyce Lednum
Certified Registered Nurse
University of Texas

"I see this book as something to have in my back-pocket."

— Adrian Gillem
Lead Engineer
Booz Allen Hamilton

Table of Contents

Introduction

Do you want to be a happier and more effective person? Of course you do!

In this book you will learn how to *debug your brain*. You will end up with a mental model of your mind and techniques to help adjust how it works. The brain techniques in this book will help you become more aware of yourself and choose the best response for a given situation.

It is especially difficult to choose a positive response when you are experiencing a *downward spiral*: a troublesome feedback loop where you feel worse and worse. Downward spirals often happen in high-stakes or emotional situations. This book covers how to notice when a downward spiral is happening, and how to defuse it.

What is debugging? Debugging means finding problems and fixing them. In the 1940s when there were room-sized computers sometimes this meant literal bugs in the computer causing issues. Once the bugs were physically removed, the computer program would work again. In today's programming terms, "bug" refers to any problem that can be fixed by editing code, and "debugging" is the process of fixing issues in the code. Thankfully, the modern use of the term has nothing to do with insects!

In the mind, debugging still means identifying and fixing problems. Debugging is the process of identifying and adjusting your mental habits, turning unhelpful thought patterns into helpful ones. This book covers techniques to help you become aware of your mental habits and learn how to adjust any unhelpful ones.

Debugging is like trying to find your way in a maze. Imagine being lost in a maze and you come across a ladder. From the top of the ladder you can see the layout of the maze much more clearly. You can see where you have been, where you intend to go, and how you can get there. There are often several paths that go to your destination. Some are shorter and direct, and others are twisty and easy to get lost in.

Sometimes it can be difficult to get this bird's eye view. You may not notice ladder-like opportunities all around you, moments where you can zoom out and take stock of the situation. Even if you do notice, it can be tricky to get yourself to pause for a moment even if it will save you time overall. If this moment of debugging can help you find a better path, it is totally worth it. This is a skill. This book covers how you can debug more readily.

About the Author

Who is writing this? Hi, I'm Casey! I studied neurobiology at Yale University, where I co-authored several neurobiology papers[1]. I have also worked in software development for 10 years.

Book Overview

Debugging Your Brain brings together two parts of my background: psychology and software development. This book is different from other applied psychology and self-help books in two ways. It concisely covers a wide range of practical techniques backed by psychology research, and it leverages software development metaphors.

Debugging Your Brain is written to be read in order, with each chapter building on the last. Each chapter is also written such that you can return to any chapter later as a reference for yourself. Each of the eight chapters covers one major concept:

1. **Introduction**, the current chapter, describes an overview of the book and describes several example scenarios to keep in mind while reading the book.
2. **Modeling the Brain** introduces a discrete mental model of how your mind works, especially around

[1]Stephanie A. Maddox et al., "A Naturally-Occurring Histone Acetyltransferase Inhibitor Derived from Garcinia Indica Impairs Newly Acquired and Reactivated Fear Memories," *PloS One* 8, no. 1 (2013): e54463, https://doi.org/10.1371/journal.pone.0054463; Stephanie A. Maddox, Casey S. Watts, and Glenn E. Schafe, "P300/CBP Histone Acetyltransferase Activity Is Required for Newly Acquired and Reactivated Fear Memories in the Lateral Amygdala," *Learning & Memory (Cold Spring Harbor, N.Y.)* 20, no. 2 (January 17, 2013): 109–19, https://doi.org/10.1101/lm.029157.112; Stephanie A. Maddox, Casey S. Watts, and Glenn E. Schafe, "DNA Methyltransferase Activity Is Required for Memory-Related Neural Plasticity in the Lateral Amygdala," *Neurobiology of Learning and Memory* 107 (January 2014): 93–100, https://doi.org/10.1016/j.nlm.2013.11.008.

thoughts and emotions.

3. **Cognitive Behavioral Therapy** (CBT) introduces the principles of this most commonly used talk therapy.
4. **Introspection** covers how to get into a mental state to effectively work with your thoughts and feelings.
5. **Identifying Inputs** describes several specific types of inputs to your brain.
6. **Experience Processing** covers principles and techniques you can use to more deeply understand your experiences.
7. **Validation** covers techniques you can use to help someone feel like their experiences are valid and understandable, which is critical to dealing with them effectively.
8. **Cognitive Restructuring** covers the most common unhelpful thought patterns, and how to counter them. This is the core idea of CBT.

You will learn the most if you can integrate these concepts into your life. Once you are aware of them, you can begin to practice and internalize them. Each chapter has activities at the end to help make this easier.

The book ends with two sections: "Key Takeaways" which summarizes the high level concepts from each chapter of this book again, and "More Resources" which points you to more ways you can dig into these techniques even more deeply.

Applying These Techniques

When can you apply these techniques? Either in the moment it is happening, if you catch yourself, or after the fact when you can reflect back on the situation. You might be able to change the outcome of the current situation, or you might at least set yourself up to have a more desirable outcome if a similar situation arises in the future.

Here are three examples of situations where this book's techniques would help. If you went through any of these totally on autopilot, you may end up with an undesirable outcome. Later we will get into what you might do to make yourself more effective in each of these, leading to a more desirable outcome.

Example 1: Work Disagreement

Imagine you are at work and you have an idea, and your coworker has a different idea. You do not agree. You are having an argument, and it gets heated. You both believe very strongly that your idea is the best one for the situation. Hopefully your team will end up making the choice that is best for the situation. This topic will likely come up again — what can you do better next time?

Example 2: Snapping as a Parent

Imagine you are a parent, and your kids forgot to shut the front door — again! You snap at them. You later feel guilty for snapping. It was not the most effective way to change their behavior in the future, and they got upset right back at you. You know you could have done something differently, but it was hard to in the moment.

Example 3: Attending An Event

Imagine you are headed to a tech event. You have not eaten dinner yet and there will be no pizza at the tech event. It is raining. You step in a puddle. You think to yourself "everything is the worst." All of a sudden you can not imagine going to the tech event anymore.

That third example happened to me! It would have been a shame to miss the event, because I was really looking forward to it. I managed to catch myself in the moment. I told myself that my wet/hungry state could both easily be fixed, and I convinced myself to go. I am glad I managed to debug my brain!

Suggested Activities

1. Think about times in your past where you wish you would have behaved differently. Come up with three specific experiences, and reflect on those as you go through this book.
2. Going forward, stay alert for more opportunities where you can leverage these skills.

Modeling The Brain

Inner versus Outer Brain

Throughout this book we will lean on a certain dichotomy of the brain. Not the left-brain versus right-brain split that is prolific in popular culture, but the inner brain versus outer brain.

Some people believe left-brained people are more inclined to be creative, and right-brained people are more inclined to be analytical. Analytical versus creative may be an interesting dichotomy, but the differences between these two halves of the brain are often exaggerated.[2] A much more useful dichotomy is the inner brain (limbic system) versus the outer brain (cerebral cortex).

To illustrate the difference between the inner and outer brain, imagine you are walking in the woods and you see — a snake!! You jump back in shock, heart racing, eyes wide. A moment later, you realize it was not actually a snake,

[2]Dahlia W. Zaidel, "Split-Brain, the Right Hemisphere, and Art: Fact and Fiction," *Progress in Brain Research* 204 (2013): 3–17, https://doi.org/10.1016/B978-0-444-63287-6.00001-4.

it was just a stick. You experienced a quick emotional reaction (which could have saved your life!) and then a slower, more thoughtful reaction in which you realized there was no actual threat.

This snake or stick scenario is the textbook example for the *Dual Pathway Model of Fear*[3]. In this model, a fear experience takes two paths in the brain: the faster *low road* and the slower *high road*.

The low road processes emotions very quickly, on the scale of milliseconds. It only has to go through the inner brain, which is a much shorter path. In evolutionary terms, the inner brain is older than the outer brain; more animals have it.

The high road is much slower. Thoughts are processed more slowly, on the scale of seconds. It has to go all the way through the outer brain, which is a much longer path. The cerebral cortex is the part of the brain which humans think thoughts in.

To summarize, feelings are processed much more quickly than thoughts. We tend to feel first and think second. We covered fear as one clear example here, but this fast versus slow dichotomy applies to many systems in the brain[4]. To remember the distinction, you can rely on the two mnemonics we covered: the snake-or-stick example, and the inner brain versus outer brain dichotomy. If you are curious to dig into nuances more, consider

---

[3]David N. Silverstein and Martin Ingvar, "A Multi-Pathway Hypothesis for Human Visual Fear Signaling," *Frontiers in Systems Neuroscience* 9 (2015): 101, https://doi.org/10.3389/fnsys.2015.00101.

[4]Keith E. Stanovich and Richard F. West, "Individual Differences in Reasoning: Implications for the Rationality Debate?" *Behavioral and Brain Sciences* October 2000, no. 23(5) (n.d.): 645–65.

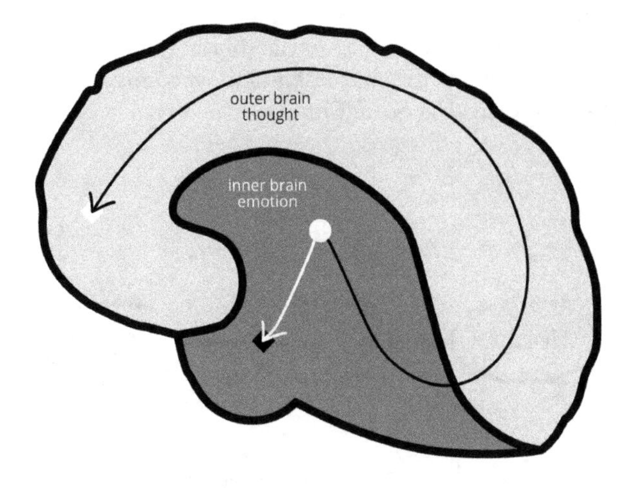

Figure 1: In the Dual Pathway Model of Fear, the *high road* is longer and slower. The *low road* is shorter and faster.

reading the book "Thinking Fast and Slow" by Daniel Kahneman.[5]

Systems Thinking

Input-Process-Output Model

To understand a system as complex as the human mind, it is helpful to start with a simple model, and build it up from there. One of the simplest and most common models is the input-process-output model.

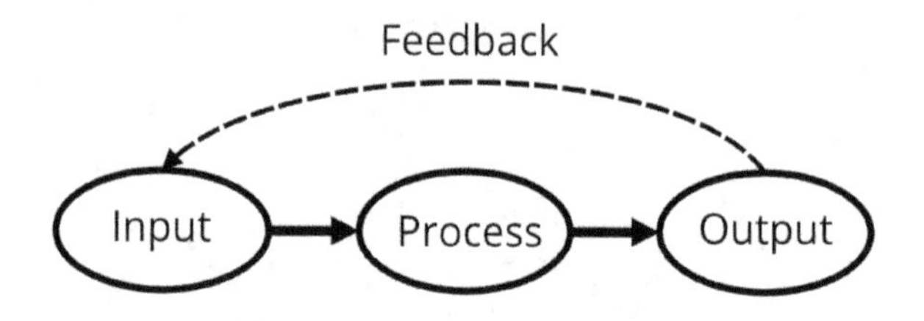

Figure 2: The input-process-output model, plus a feedback loop.

The input-process-output model, or IPO model, contains the three parts of its name: input, process, and output. Sometimes a feedback loop is also added.

A textbook example of the IPO model is the thermostat in your home.

---

[5] *Thinking, Fast and Slow*, 1st pbk. ed (New York: Farrar, Straus and Giroux, 2013).

- Input: The thermostat measures the temperature of the room.
- Process: The thermostat compares that temperature to the set temperature, determining if it is above or below the temperature you set.
- Output: The thermostat then toggles the heater on or off accordingly.
- Feedback: The temperature of the room changes, and the cycle repeats, giving a new input to the system.

Now for a software example: imagine a program that reverses the letters in a word you give it. You write "apple" and it writes back "elppa". Somewhere inside the program, it reads the input word from right to left one letter at a time, and then it returns the new word it creates. The input is "apple", the process is the transformation inside the program, and the output is "elppa". This is the IPO model!

Most actual programs are more interesting than this. Programs are often composed of many smaller "functions" that each take an input and produce an output. Many programs have hundreds or thousands or even more interrelated functions.

Systems Thinking & Conscious Thought

We can use the IPO model to model brains, too! The simplest form of this is just an input and an output. Imagine a simple model of an animal that says they do not really *think* — they just respond to their environment. This simplified model represents the animal as just inputs and outputs, ignoring what goes on in between. Here is an example:

In a classic experiment, a dog is trained to associate

a bell being rung with being fed. After many rounds of ringing the bell when the dog is fed, the dog is conditioned to associate the two. With this conditioning, every time the bell rings, the dog salivates — even when there is no food around. The dog does not have to decide whether to salivate. Salivation is an automatic reaction the dog has to an external stimulus. This phenomenon can be referred to as *Pavlovian conditioning* or *classical conditioning*.

In this oversimplified model, we can imagine there is no conscious *process* going on inside the animal, focusing instead on the inputs and outputs. In contrast, we often believe we humans always have conscious thought — that we think thoughts and feel feelings in a conscious way all of the time.

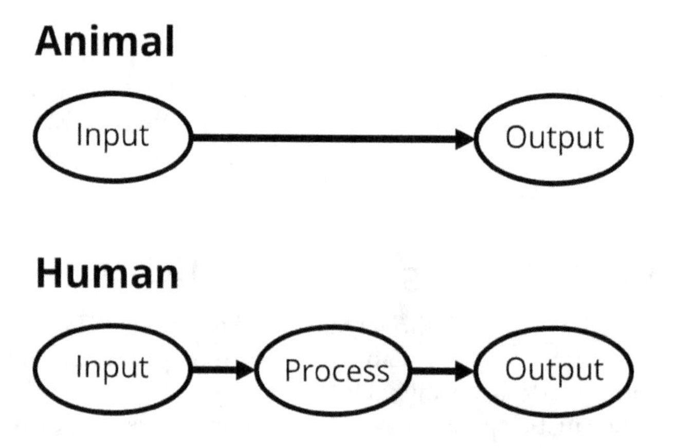

Figure 3: Model of an animal: input leads to output. Model of a human: input leads to process leads to output.

This model is perhaps too generous to humans. We humans are not always aware of what goes on inside our heads, like when we are on autopilot. When we are on *autopilot*, the earlier input-output model we used for Pavlov's dog seems more appropriate. When we are letting habits run things, the process part is not really under our control.

When we are mindful, we are not letting autopilot run things; we are consciously aware of our thoughts and feelings; we have much more influence over the process part of our mind. When we wield a mindful state, we have more influence over the output, our actions, as well.

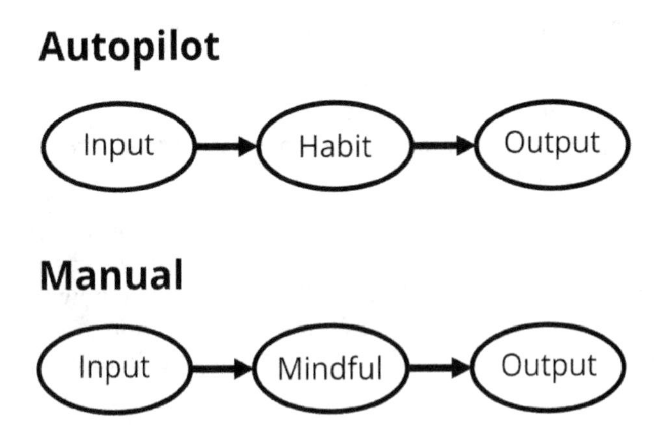

Figure 4: Model of autopilot mode: input leads to a habitual process leads to output. Model of manual mode: input leads to a mindful process leads to output.

The focus for the models we have diagrammed here is to point out that we can activate a mindful process between our inputs and outputs to consciously choose how we act.

Consciously changing our thinking patterns in this manual, mindful state can absolutely influence our habits. Once something is a habit, we do not have to think about it during every little interaction. This is the power of debugging your brain - reprogramming yourself.

Automatic and Deliberate Thoughts and Feelings

Automatic inputs are ones you cannot control, they happen "to" you. From the perspective of your consciousness *automatic thoughts* and *automatic feelings* are inputs.

When you are being mindful, you can actively choose to have *deliberate thoughts* and influence your feelings. You can probably imagine how to have a *deliberate thought* — you just think it!

Feelings are partially within your influence, but not within your direct control. You cannot will yourself to experience a specific feeling directly. You can, however, influence your feelings based on deliberate thoughts you think. This influenced-feeling is partially deliberate.

Downward Spiral

Sometimes these thoughts and feelings can cause a troublesome feedback loop — a *downward spiral*. A downward spiral is a feedback loop of negative thoughts, leading to negative feelings, leading to more negative thoughts, and so on. Both automatic ones and deliberate ones can affect this.

Automatic vs Deliberate Thoughts and Feelings

	automatic	deliberate
thought	automatic thought	deliberate thought
feeling	automatic feeling	influenced feeling

Figure 5: Table showing the relationship between automatic thoughts, automatic feelings, deliberate thoughts, and influenced feelings.

For example, that time when I stepped in a puddle on my way to a tech event. That made my already-bad mood even worse. I heard myself automatically think something like "Ugh, I'm stupid," and that kicked off a downward spiral for me.

A downward spiral like this is usually counterproductive. It makes you feel worse and it distracts you from focusing on things which are more important. We generally want to avoid downward spirals. Some exceptions are covered later in this book, like when you want to get yourself worked up to have the energy for something.

If you can effectively influence your mind, you can often control whether you let this happen to yourself or not. You will become more effective, think more clearly, and choose a better response more often.

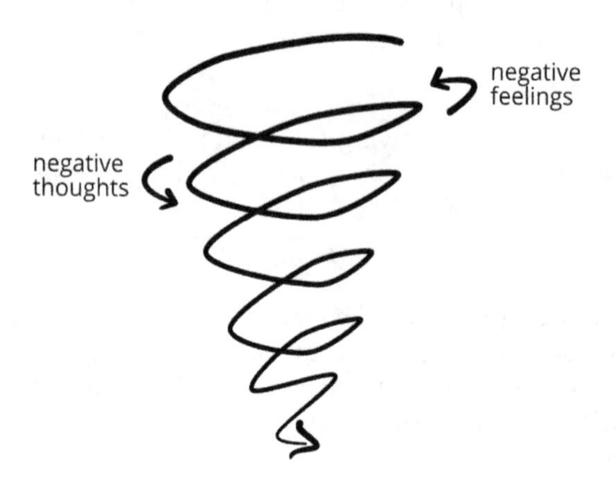

Figure 6: A downward spiral. Negative thoughts lead to negative feelings which lead back to more negative thoughts.

Suggested Activities

1. Draw out the IPO model from memory.
2. Try to explain the snake-or-stick example and the *inner brain* versus *outer brain* dichotomy to a friend or coworker.
3. Consider reading the book "Thinking Fast and Slow" by Kahneman.

Cognitive Behavioral Therapy

Cognitive Behavioral Therapy (CBT) is a specific and common form of talk therapy. Therapists know and use many different therapy approaches, and CBT is one of the most common and effective ones. CBT is effective for depression, anxiety, general stress such as from work, and much more!

The core idea is that certain patterns of thought contribute to emotional distress and behavioral issues. These *cognitive distortions* offer an inaccurate view of the world and an inaccurate view of yourself. Fortunately, cognitive distortions can be identified and corrected with practice and effort.

CBT has been shown to help with a long list of mental health issues. One study grouped these into fifteen categories, and each category had many more issues inside of them[6]. It may be more interesting to ask what CBT does

[6]The list of issues CBT has been shown to help with at least some

not help with! CBT is not necessarily the best or only therapy for each and every one of these mental issues. It is, however, one of the most frequently used techniques, and it is often very effective.

You may be wondering "Wouldn't I need a mental health issue to care about CBT?" Nope! The use of the word "therapy" here can be a bit misleading. Whether or not you have any mental health issues, CBT can help you be happier and more effective.

Therapy? Training!

Mental health is stigmatized. Although the stigma has been getting better over time, it is still a powerful force. Even if you support and encourage other people to get therapy, you may still have a natural aversion to therapy for yourself. I feel this effect, too! If you relate to this, you might like this reframing: instead of thinking "Cognitive Behavioral Therapy," try thinking of it as "Cognitive Behavioral Training." We all benefit from learning new skills, and CBT is exactly that — a skill. You can practice this skill, and you can get training for this skill.

However, if you are at all unsure whether you would

---

amount includes these: "substance use disorder, schizophrenia and other psychotic disorders, depression and dysthymia, bipolar disorder, anxiety disorders, somatoform disorders, eating disorders, insomnia, personality disorders, anger and aggression, criminal behaviors, general stress, distress due to general medical conditions, chronic pain and fatigue, distress related to pregnancy complications and female hormonal conditions", according to Stefan G. Hofmann et al., "The Efficacy of Cognitive Behavioral Therapy: A Review of Meta-Analyses," *Cognitive Therapy and Research* 36, no. 5 (October 1, 2012): 427–40, https://doi.org/10.1007/s10608-012-9476-1

benefit from or "need" actual therapy, I recommend you see someone to be screened. A therapist or even your primary care provider can ask you a series of questions to gauge how much you would benefit from therapy. There are screenings for depression, for anxiety, and many other mental health issues. A screening can be so quick that it is quite unfortunate how many people with mental health issues simply have not been screened. You may benefit from a screening.

You may want to dig in deeper on your own, whether or not you choose to get support from a healthcare professional as well. Psychology-based self-help books have been shown to be as effective as in-person therapy for many people[7]. Books are also, of course, much less expensive than in-person therapy. The term used in the research on this is "bibliotherapy," which means therapy by reading books. One particular book I would recommend as bibliotherapy is "Feeling Good: The New Mood Therapy"[8].

Positive Outcomes

There are two tangible positive outcomes from processing experiences. One is *learning*, and the other is reducing *intrusive thoughts*.

If you can learn something from a situation, that might help you in a similar one. This could be something specific

[7]M. R. Gualano et al., "The Long-Term Effects of Bibliotherapy in Depression Treatment: Systematic Review of Randomized Clinical Trials," *Clinical Psychology Review* 58 (December 2017): 49–58, https://doi.org/10.1016/j.cpr.2017.09.006.

[8]David D. Burns, *Feeling Good: The New Mood Therapy*, Rev. and updated (New York: Avon, 1999).

like "make sure you have your keys when you leave the house," or something more abstract like "try slowing down and be more careful."

Processing can also help reduce intrusive thoughts. Intrusive thoughts are unwelcome, distressing, involuntary thoughts which often happen at inappropriate times.

Imagine you recently had a job interview. After the interview you were not sure how it went, and you think about it a lot. You play back what everyone said and did, thinking about what you could have done differently. Thinking about this experience more is probably some amount helpful, and some amount unhelpful. If these stressful thoughts continue happening to you out of nowhere, these are intrusive thoughts.

How can you put intrusive thoughts to rest? There are two ways: find value, or find acceptance. You can find value in the experience by learning something from it. What can you do now that it is over? What can you do differently next time? If you cannot learn anything further from the intrusive thoughts, it may help to accept the situation[9]. You cannot change how the interview went once it is over. Finding value or finding acceptance can help reduce the frequency and intensity of intrusive thoughts.

---

[9]Adrian Wells and Panagiotis Roussis, "Refraining from Intrusive Thoughts Is Strategy Dependent: A Comment on Sugiura, et Al. And a Preliminary Informal Test of Detached Mindfulness, Acceptance, and Other Strategies," *Psychological Reports* 115, no. 2 (October 2014): 541–44, https://doi.org/10.2466/02.PR0.115c21z9.

Suggested Activities

1. Explain CBT at a high level to a friend. Do a bit of independent research if you want to be able to speak about it more accurately.
2. Consider being screened for any mental health issues, today while you are thinking about it.
3. Try to notice any intrusive thoughts you experience this week. Think about what might help reduce their frequency: learning, or acceptance.

Introspection

Hitting Your Debugger

When can you process an experience? It could be during, immediately after, hours after, weeks after, or even years after. How do we get into an introspective state to do this processing/debugging? It depends on whether you are debugging during or after the stressful situation. Each is valuable in its own way.

After a Situation

When you debug your brain after an experience, you may learn things which can help you in a similar situation in the future. This post-processing can also help reduce how often you think of the situation and how stressful it is to think about. Of course, it also prepares you to better handle the situation next time.

During a Situation

If you are able to debug your brain during a stressful situation, you may be able to change the outcome of that situation. You may also be able to make this current experience a less stressful one.

Many people find it difficult to realize when it is a good opportunity to introspect in-moment. We will go through a technique in the next chapter to help with noticing opportunities for introspection and getting you into that introspective mindset.

The Whoop Technique

Example Opportunity

To start up your debugger in the moment, I recommend the *whoop technique.*

I came up with this technique with my mother. One day, she snapped at my younger brother for leaving the door open. Immediately after, she felt bad and apologized. She told us she really did not know why she yelled about "such a small thing." After thinking about it for a bit, she realized she had not eaten that day. She was pretty hungry. That hunger affected her mood and it affected and her response to my brother. After she ate something, she felt much less irritable. I really am very proud of her for introspecting and learning like this. She even told us about it as it was going on — great job, mom!

Whoop!

This was not the first or last time this sort of thing would happen. My mother wanted to get better at this — better at noticing things like how her hunger, thoughts, and emotions could affect her mood. Once she got into an introspective state she could figure it out well enough, but she had trouble getting into an introspective state in the first place.

My mom asked us to help her next time she got frustrated or upset like this. We brainstormed together, and decided that next time we could loudly yell "WHOOP!" After the whoop, she might think to enter an introspective state (the *whoop state*) and try processing the experience. Or if she does not want to introspect right now, she could say "not now" and we would move on. She whoops herself, I whoop myself, my brother whoops himself. We all whoop!

Figure 7: The Whoop Technique in three stages: Problem, Whoop, and then the Whoop State.

I do not always yell whoop out loud. When I do yell

whoop out loud that can be more powerful at getting my attention, but sometimes it is not appropriate. When I cannot or do not want to whoop out loud I instead think in my head, loudly.

This technique is most useful for whooping yourself. If you want to recruit friends or family to support you that is great, but definitely optional.

Whether it is silent or out loud, a whoop surprises you out of your current mindset. If you were about to spiral downward, it halts that for a moment. It puts you into a different mental state where you can be ready to think about what made you so frustrated in the first place. For my mom, her frustration was not really about what my brother was doing in particular, her hunger was a much bigger factor. We will cover more inputs which might affect your mood later in this chapter.

It will take practice for you to get good at noticing opportunities where introspection will help. Just being able to notice these opportunities is a huge step forward. Whenever you get into this introspective state (*whoop state*), I want you to congratulate yourself. You will get better and better the more you do this. Be patient with yourself in the meantime.

Post-hoc Rationalization

When my brother did not close the door, my mom stopped to introspect for a moment. If she had not, she might have explained her behavior in an unsatisfying, inaccurate way called a *post-hoc rationalization*. Post-hoc means "after the fact." We often experience a gut reaction first (inner brain), and then afterwards attempt to explain our thoughts and feelings soon after (outer brain). Often the first attempt at explaining it is inaccurate or incomplete. This could cause internal conflict for yourself, or conflict with others.

Some blatant examples my mom may have thought include: "he always does that!" (even if he has not done it much) and "he's going to let all the heat out!" (even if the heat was off). Post-hoc rationalization can happen during or after a situation, whether the situation is stressful or not. It can happen anytime.

When you find yourself experiencing this, take a moment to introspect. Your first explanation may be inaccurate, but your gut feeling is likely rooted in reality in some way. By spending time processing you may be able to come up with a fuller, more satisfying explanation for yourself and for others. Whoop!

Breakpoint Metaphor

When we whoop and enter the whoop state, we are pausing the running program that is our mind. Once it is paused, we can see what is going on and potentially intervene. It is interrupting the automatic processing with manual intervention.

In programming terms, a whoop moment is like hitting a debugger *breakpoint*. When programming, sometimes you want to see what is going on in the middle of a running program. You can mark where in the code you want to pause the program by using a certain code word like "breakpoint". Once you are finished debugging inside that breakpoint, you then tell the program to *continue*.

Earlier in the book we described a function which reverses the order of letters in a word, like from "apple" to "elppa". If you wanted to see what is going on in the running program, you could set a debugger breakpoint inside of this function and then start the program. Once it gets to that point, the program would pause at the debugger breakpoint, giving manual control over to you, the programmer.

From this breakpoint you can ask the computer questions like "what inputs did this function get?". You can try out new code from inside here to see how it would work. You could even change the output of the function during this one run of the program, and see how that affects other parts of the program. Once you are finished working with the breakpoint, you can signal for the program to continue running.

When Not to Whoop?

It takes both time and energy to introspect. If you do not have the time or energy to introspect as much as you would like, that is okay and normal. Sometimes you may enter the "whoop" state briefly, decide it is not worth introspecting right now, and leave before processing things. If it feels right to skip going deeper, that is totally okay.

You want to prevent most downward spirals. They are often a waste of your time and energy, or lead to actions you may regret. However, sometimes it might be worth it to let yourself get worked up. You may be driven to focus on something you would not otherwise.

Example

Story time! Once I had a bad experience in a food court. I was eating a meal, charging my phone, when a security officer rudely told me I could not use the power outlet. I felt myself getting worked up, I whooped internally, and I entered an introspective state. I considered — should I control my thoughts and feelings and prevent myself from being worked up? In this case, I decided to allow this to motivate me to act.

I was energized enough to talk to the manager of the food court and make my thoughts known. I wanted to help future people who needed to charge their phone. And for the food court's sake, I wanted the management to have this information they would not otherwise get. I wanted to explain: it cost virtually nothing to the company (literally <$0.001 for a full phone charge). I was not in the way of anything. I was not taking up needed space (the food court was empty). There was no sign up about this rule anywhere, and the person asking me to unplug was rude about it.

I introspected enough to be able to describe my experience clearly, but not so much as to diffuse my motivation. I want this information (the story of my experience) to make it to someone who could potentially do something about it. If they don't have access to this information, how could they make it better? I am proud to be someone who can calmly and clearly share context like this, and then let it go. I do not expect other people to feel this way, but I often feel compelled to share context like this.

You can become very skilled at introspection and still allow yourself to get worked up sometimes. You do not need to always mechanically control your thoughts.

Imagine you are now an expert at using the whoop technique to get into an introspective state. What can you do next? We'll cover that in the next few chapters.

Suggested Activities

1. Practice the "whoop." Find three moments today where you could be more introspective, and try out the whoop. This could be silent or out loud.
2. Identify some times you did "post-hoc rationalization" in the past week, or keep a look-out for ones you do in the next few days. What inaccurate summaries did you make? How can you rephrase those to be more accurate?

Identifying Inputs

So you can whoop yourself, now what? The next few chapters cover what actions you can take in this whoop state, in input-process-output order. This chapter "Identifying Inputs" will be about taking stock of the inputs to your mind. The following three chapters go more in-depth on processing. Two chapters about processing feelings, "Experience Processing" and "Experience Validation". One chapter is about processing thoughts, "Cognitive Distortions".

Once you have worked through the "I" and the "P", you are then well equipped to affect the "O" of IPO. You now have information you need to choose a more adaptive response, better than your autopilot alone could do.

Four Inputs

There are at least four categories of input to your system:

1. automatic feelings
2. automatic thoughts
3. external stimuli

4. current bodily state

Automatic Feelings

Any feelings you experience are a type of input. A feeling can be present whether you can accurately describe it in words or not. A feeling can sometimes come with automatic thoughts describing it, but sometimes a feeling does not come with automatic thoughts.

You may experience a feeling in a particular moment like a moment of fear, or you may experience a longer running background feeling like being anxious for a day or a month. The specific distinction between these is not super important — it is more important that you scan yourself for both kinds.

Some people make a distinction between *feelings* which we are consciously aware of and *emotions* which are not necessarily felt. For this book we will use the terms as synonyms. Our goal in either case is to be aware of them and be able to describe them.

Automatic Thoughts

An automatic thought is one you do not actively choose to think. You just "hear" the thought as it appears in your head. My mom automatically thought the words "Oh, not again!" This automatic thought came to her around the same time as an *automatic feeling* of frustration. Both automatic feelings and automatic thoughts are inputs to the conscious part of your brain. These are not directly under your control.

External Stimuli

An external stimulus is anything that happens outside of your body or mind. Often these are events that happen around you, like my younger brother not shutting the door. It could be some event from earlier in the day, like if you wake up late or miss a cup of coffee. It could be something someone said to you the day, month, or year before. These events happening to you are separate from any thoughts or feelings you have about them.

Bodily State

A fourth type of input is your current bodily state. My favorite example is a portmanteau, a word that is a combination of other words. The word *hangry* is a portmanteau of hungry and angry. If you are hangry, that means your state of hunger is leading you to experience anger, and you may respond to the situation with anger. When my mom realized she had not eaten, she apologized to my brother, moved on, and got some food.

Hangry has become a common term lately, and I would love to have an even richer vocabulary with words like this. I have not come up with any mashup words that are quite as catchy as *hangry*, but hyphenation helps me a lot. I have considered pushing for "tiredrated" to catch on, but I hyphenate it instead: tired-frustrated. Any [bodily-state]-[emotional-state] combination is a possibility. Try making your own!

For myself, I even distinguish between many types of hungry: low blood sugar hungry, low stomach volume hungry, craving hungry, mouth hungry, thirsty hungry, and bored hungry[10]. I also distinguish between many types of tired (physically tired, sleepy-tired, socially drained, and focused-for-too-long drained).

Those are four types of input: automatic feelings, automatic thoughts, stimuli from the environment, and current bodily state. Now equipped with all this context, we are ready to start processing these thoughts and emotions.

Suggested Activities

1. Think of a time when you could have used brain debugging, and identify what inputs you had in that situation. Consider all four types of input.
2. Come up with a term of your own which describes how your bodily state affects your emotional state, like hangry or the hyphenated term "tired-frustrated."

[10]Casey S. Watts, "Six Types of Hunger," Blog, Casey Watts Blog, December 18, 2017, https://caseywatts.com/2017/12/18/types-of-hunger.html.

Experience Processing

In this chapter, "Experience Processing," you will learn techniques to help you process experiences by putting them into words. Verbalizing can help you better understand your experiences, and express them to others. Verbalizing experiences can help reduce the stress you feel about a given situation, making you feel more in control and at ease. It can help you choose the best response for the current situation or a future one.

First we will cover three principles, and then we will dig into six techniques that leverage those principles. We will start with these three principles: 1. verbalizing your experiences 2. avoiding rumination 3. accepting automatic inputs as data

The Three Principles

Verbalizing Your Experiences

Putting an experience into words can be a huge relief, especially when the experience is complex or troublesome.

Words give us handles we can use to hold onto aspects of the experience. We can use these to investigate and figure out what is really going on. By using accurate language, we can process experiences a lot more deeply and effectively than we can by using abstract, wordless thoughts alone. You might verbalize an experience by thinking to yourself, by talking to a friend, or by writing.

Avoiding Rumination

When processing thoughts and feelings, there is a risk of accidentally ruminating on them instead of effectively processing them.

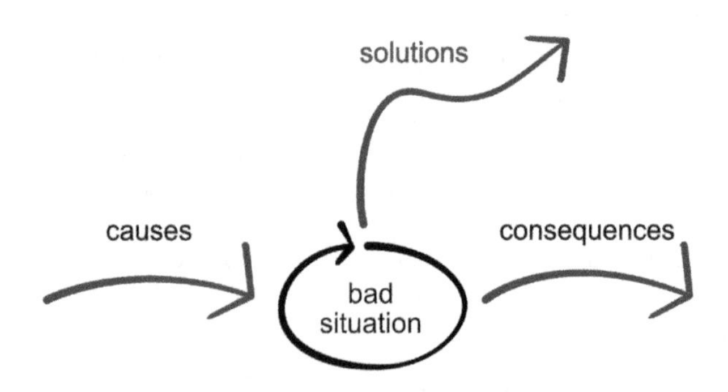

Figure 8: Rumination is focusing on the causes and consequences of a problem, instead of on its potential solutions.

Rumination is focusing on the causes and consequences

of a problem, instead of on its potential solutions. When you are too focused on the negative, it may cause a downward spiral and make you feel even worse. If you notice yourself ruminating, you may want to take a break and try again later. If you are not careful, you could accidentally reinforce maladaptive thought patterns.

Earlier we covered an example of rumination without calling it rumination - focusing on an interview where you are not sure how it went. It can be easy to accidentally focus too much on what things may have gone wrong during the interview, and imagining all the potential negative consequences. It can be challenging to think of constructive things that would help your situation, like sending a thank you note. With practice, you can learn to notice when you are accidentally ruminating, and instead focus on being constructive.

Accepting Automatic Inputs as Data

In our input-process-output model of the mind, automatic thoughts and automatic feelings are inputs to your system. To avoid rumination, strive to accept your automatic thoughts and automatic feelings as inputs. Accept these inputs as data, without judgment.

When you accept automatic inputs as data, you can process them more fully. When you instead fixate on them and judge them, that can be very counterproductive. Ruminating on and judging inputs may even *cause* a downward spiral.

This skill of non-judgmentally accepting inputs as data gets easier with practice. To actively work on this, try meditation. Meditation practice is, at the core, training your brain so it focuses on observing thoughts and emotions instead of judging them.

Six Techniques

Those three principles were verbalizing, avoiding rumination, and accepting inputs as data. Next we will cover six concrete techniques that leverage those principles:

1. talk with a friend
2. talk with a rubber duck
3. write
4. meditate
5. read fiction
6. expand your emotional vocabulary

Talk with a Friend

Talking through an experience with a close friend is one of the most powerful processing techniques. This is also my personal favorite. Not only is it helpful for processing the experience, but this is also a bonding opportunity for your relationship.

In order to communicate your thoughts and feelings to another person, you have to put them into concrete words. If your friend can accurately reflect back to you what you are saying, that helps you be more confident you are understandable. This confidence can help you feel more settled about that part of the experience. This can help you move on to processing other details.

Sometimes a friend will describe something in a different way than you would. If you like their phrasing, you might adopt it yourself. When you sometimes have trouble putting an idea into words, a friend can help you explore those. They might brainstorm different ways of describing it until something feels accurate and correct. If you especially like a particular phrasing you might even write it down to reference later.

Here is an example of how I process experiences with a friend.

1. First, I check for availability. I ask the friend if they can help me talk through something. This makes sure they are available to help me process my unprocessed thoughts before diving in. I want to make sure they have time and are also willing to do the emotional labor involved.
2. Then, I share my experience with them. When sharing unprocessed thoughts, sometimes I end up rambling a bit. It can take a few tries to figure out the right word. For example, I might try: "I feel good about it. Excited maybe? Not quite excited. I do think it'll go my way, and that's a comforting feeling."
3. As we go through the experience, sometimes we brainstorm together. When I am having trouble describing something, my actively-listening friend might suggest some phrasing for me, like "are you feeling confident?" If they are right, we have named this feeling! If not, we can continue on until some description feels right. Often you can find a single word for something. If not, you can at least find a phrase or sentence-long explanation of the feeling.

If your friend can reflect back to you accurately how you are feeling, that can make you feel understood. It can be very comforting and validating. This can help you move on, now that the experience has been processed.

Talking with a friend is often the most powerful method of processing an experience, but talking with an unsupportive friend could make you feel worse. A friend might inadvertently invalidate your experiences, making you feel more uncertain about them.

You cannot control how effectively your friend supports you, but you can influence it some. Even if you talk about how you want to be supported explicitly, it can be hard for them. Supporting other people is a skill.

If you can be a good model of active listening and effective validation, it may help your friends learn how to support you in a helpful way. When you are listening to friends, there are many tactics you can use yourself to make them feel validated, which we cover later in this book.

Talk With a Rubber Duck

Not ready to talk to a friend? Try a rubber duck!

Our second technique is a common software development trick: "rubber duck debugging". This is often taught in introduction to programming courses. They suggest: put a rubber duck on your desk, or imagine one. Pretend the duck is sentient and explain the situation to it. Imagine what questions it would ask, and what information it would need to know to be able to help. You can have a full-on conversation with this duck whether it is out loud, in your head, or in writing.

Often by talking to a rubber duck I end up not needing

to ask for help from anyone else at all! The process of verbalizing how to describe my issue helps reveal what assumptions I am making. The root of my problem often lies somewhere in those assumptions. Enunciating those assumptions really helps make the situation clearer.

You could imagine the duck has similar context to a coworker, or someone else like your manager, your best friend, a family member, etc. And if you cannot think of an existing person who would be particularly appropriate, you can even imagine up someone new. What context would this imagined person need to be able to help you work through this?

This rubber duck technique may not seem effective at first glance. I am still surprised myself at how often it works. It really does.

Duck or Friend

Sometimes you may talk through a situation with your rubber duck and still want to talk to a friend afterwards. Talking to the rubber duck helps you do a certain level of processing, putting your experience into words as much as you can on your own. Later when you are with your friend, you can express yourself much more clearly. Together with your friend, you can dig in even deeper than you could have been able to otherwise.

Before meeting with your friend, think of what questions that friend would need to ask to get context. Think about what assumptions you are making that would be helpful to make explicit. The more you can enunciate on your own, the smoother and deeper a discussion with a friend will go.

Write

Writing is the third technique. Writing can help you go even deeper on an issue than just talking or thinking. Writing activates a different part of the brain, and makes you really nail down thoughts and feelings. When you take time to write, you can also focus more on the words you are using.

To start, you might "brainstorm," writing down everything in a stream-of-consciousness way. Just putting your thoughts and feelings into words, even if they are not very accurate to start. After brainstorming, you can then re-read and edit it until it feels accurate. Some parts will likely feel "off" on your first try, and you can iterate on them. Try to use the most specific words you can, especially for emotions.

I use the term **journaling** to mean "writing out thoughts and feelings," wherever and whenever that is. This is useful even if you do not write those thoughts and feelings in a notebook by your bedside every day.

Some people write in a notebook on their bedside table every day, but that is not the only way to journal. You do not even need a physical journal to practice journaling. Some people prefer writing on a computer or phone. My favorite place to journal is in an email draft message. It is quick to load and does not have any frills to get in the way. Often I will start an email draft imagining I would send it to a coworker (but with my name in the "to:" to be safe).

You can write to yourself, future-you, past-you, or to the journal itself. You could write to your rubber duck, your best friend, or anyone.

Meditate

Practicing meditation can help you become more aware of your thoughts and emotions. Unlike many of the other techniques, meditation is not great for actively thinking about and processing experiences. Meditation is useful for becoming aware of thoughts and feelings in the first place and accepting them as inputs, so you can process them later.

If you would like to try getting into meditation, there are a lot of resources to help you get started in a gentle and gradual way. My favorite introduction to meditation is a mobile app, "Headspace." It introduces meditation concepts one at a time, using voice guidance and cute little video animations.

One risk with meditation is rumination, focusing on negative causes and consequences in a way that makes you feel worse. Sitting with these thoughts and feelings which you are normally unaware of can be stressful. Stress is more likely to happen in a particularly challenging situation, or when you are mentally or bodily fatigued. It is easy to judge these and accidentally kick off a downward spiral, making yourself feel worse. This risk is especially high for beginners. With practice, you will get better at not judging your thoughts and feelings during meditation.

Read Fiction

Some people believe nonfiction reading is more useful than fiction reading, but both are useful in their own way. Nonfiction books may teach facts, but fiction books are useful for social and emotional development.

Reading fiction helps you imagine how other people think. Fiction books give you the opportunity to peer inside another person's mind. Often, their thoughts and feelings are different or at least articulated differently than you would experience in a similar situation. From reading, you get to see how the characters deal with situations, how they interact with others, and the results of those interactions. The characters often act in ways we would not ourselves, and in situations we could never find ourselves in.

The only way an author is able to convey these thoughts and feelings is to use words. If you can pick up on their wording or vocabulary that can help with your own wording and vocabulary.

Some research has been done on this phenomenon, using the theory of *narrative transportation*. The term *high emotional transportation* means a story where the reader imagines they are immersed in the world, connecting and empathizing with the characters. Some studies show that people who have recently read books with "high emotional transportation" have greater empathy than those who read something without high emotional transportation[11].

Try reading some fiction! You do not need to read from a high school English class curriculum; today's popular fiction totally counts. If you need an idea, maybe start with something from the top 10 bestsellers list for this year. You probably even know some people who have read some of these popular books, and you can bond over that.

---

[11] P. Matthijs Bal and Martijn Veltkamp, "How Does Fiction Reading Influence Empathy? An Experimental Investigation on the Role of Emotional Transportation," *PloS One* 8, no. 1 (2013): e55341, https://doi.org/10.1371/journal.pone.0055341

Expand Your Emotional Vocabulary

Children are usually taught the simplest emotions first, like happy, sad, angry, tired. Later they learn how to describe more complex emotions. There are many more words available than you likely regularly use, but with practice you can incorporate this vocabulary into your everyday use.

Enriching your vocabulary can help you with both automatic and deliberate thoughts and feelings. The more accurate vocabulary you use in your deliberate thoughts, the more you will start to use this vocabulary automatically. Each small nudge in the right direction adds up. Each thought you deliberately think helps influence your thinking habits.

To expand your emotional vocabulary, use a thesaurus or a visual diagram like an "emotions wheel". One resource I recommend in particular is the Wikipedia article on "emotion classification,"[12] which lists many interesting ways to think about emotions. There are many different scales that emotions are plotted on from low to high. Some are modeled in a circular diagram, some are in a tree structure list with primary, secondary, tertiary levels of emotional complexity from branches out to leaves. Some are even modeled using equations.

The next time you are trying to describe your emotions, whether to yourself or to someone else, try using a reference. You may find a certain word that is a little more accurate than what you would think of naturally. You might also ask a friend how they would describe it.

---

[12]https://en.wikipedia.org/wiki/Emotion_classification

Suggested Activities

1. Find and print out an emotional vocabulary chart, like one from the Wikipedia page for "Emotion Classification". Put it somewhere handy so you can easily find it when you need it: print it, or save it to your desktop, or email it to yourself.
2. Try processing emotions a bit each day this week. Try a different tactic each day, including:
   a. Schedule a time with a friend to talk about your feelings
   b. Discuss a problem with a "rubber duck" for 10 minutes
   c. Journal for 10 minutes once
   d. Meditate for at least three sessions, perhaps using an app like Headspace[13] or Calm[14].
3. Choose a fiction book to read. An audiobook counts just as well.

[13]https://www.headspace.com/
[14]https://www.calm.com/

Experience Validation

This chapter focuses on how you can use validation techniques to help other people feel supported. You can help your friends process their experiences by validating their experiences, especially their inputs. This also helps your friends learn to support you better when you can model the kind of support you would like to receive. These validation techniques also apply to self-validation, but I find it easier to practice explicit validation on other people to start. The examples in this chapter will be focused on validating other people's experiences.

Close Relationships

There is a "loneliness epidemic" in the US lately[15]. So many people do not have enough close relationships to provide the social and emotional support support that we all need.

[15]Ellie Polack, "New Cigna Study Reveals Loneliness at Epidemic Levels in America," Cigna, a Global Health Insurance and Health Service Company, accessed July 19, 2020, https://www.cigna.com/newsroom/news-releases/2018/new-cigna-study-reveals-loneliness-at-epidemic-levels-in-america.

The more close connections you have, the healthier you are, the longer you live, and the more resilient you are in the face of stress. The list of positive benefits of social connectedness goes on and on.

One of the best ways you can address this yourself is to have more high-quality relationships[16]. Consider making it a priority to cultivate deeper relationships. It can be difficult, but it is well worth the effort.

Being safely vulnerable with each other can deepen feelings of trust. This can dramatically improve your relationship. This goes in both directions: you want friends who can support you, and you should be willing to support your friends as well. One of the most powerful support skills is communicating validation and acceptance, covered in the next section.

Communicating Validation

To help friends feel emotionally supported, we want them to feel validated — to feel understood. Validation means to accept another person's thoughts and feelings as understandable, even if we would not have thought the same things or felt the same way ourselves. It can be difficult to explicitly communicate validation to a friend, but it is a skill you can learn and practice. My favorite framework for thinking about validation is Dr. Marcia Linehan's "Six Levels of Validation."

[16]Marissa King, "Working to Address the Loneliness Epidemic: Perspective-Taking, Presence, and Self-Disclosure," *American Journal of Health Promotion* 32, no. 5 (June 2018): 1315–7, https://doi.org/10.1177/0890117118776735c.

This is not a strict scale of what you should use when, you will have to determine what is best based on your context. The six levels of validation is a framework to use when considering how to respond to a friend who is being vulnerable with you. Here are the six levels of validation, from lowest impact to highest impact:

1. Be Present
2. Accurate Reflection
3. Guessing at Unstated Feelings
4. Validate Based on the Past
5. Validate Based on Today
6. Radical Genuineness

1 - Be Present

The first level of validation is just being present, even if you are not saying anything to each other. Sometimes a friend may not be ready to dig in to talking about something yet. Sometimes a situation is too difficult or tiring to talk about, or a wound too fresh and painful. Your presence alone can have a validating impact. Physical presence may have a stronger effect than being present over the phone or text, but any form of presence can have this sort of effect some amount.

2 - Accurate Reflection

The second level of validation is accurate reflection. When your friend feels understood, that is very validating. If you can accurately describe your friend's thoughts and feelings back to them, that shows you understand them. This is especially powerful if you can internalize what they are saying enough to put it into your own words. Even if you can only echo their words back to them, that can still show you are listening and trying to understand.

3 - Guessing About Unstated Feelings

If your friend has not communicated something clearly or fully enough yet, perhaps you can help. Your friend could feel very understood if you can suggest an accurate way of describing how they feel.

Sometimes you may even describe things in a way which inspires a change in the way they think about the situation. They may have new words to apply to the situation, both in their mind and out loud. Effectively guessing about unstated feelings is generally more validating than just being present or just accurately reflecting.

Be careful with this level, though. It can be very tricky to guess about unstated feelings. There is a fine balance between conveying your understanding, and leaving space to be corrected. It is the difference between helping your friend refine their wording versus imposing your own wording on them.

If you do not guess enough to convey your understanding, you may miss an opportunity for validation. However, if you guess incorrectly and without room for correction, that can be actively invalidating. This can leave your friend feeling misunderstood, and leave you with an uncorrected, incorrect guess. To misunderstand someone is worse than just not understanding them. It is tough to balance conveying your understanding with leaving room for correction.

I have two tools I use when trying to be an effective guesser of unstated feelings. One is the open-closed spectrum, and the other is the confidence level spectrum. Both of these apply to each statement, observation, and question you make. These two tools can help you balance conveying your understanding against leaving room for correction. First we will go through the open-closed spectrum with an explanation and examples, and then we will go through the confidence level spectrum the same way.

Open-closed Spectrum

The open-closed spectrum ranges from open-ended questions and statements to closed-ended ones. An open-ended question like "how did that make you feel?" is very good at encouraging your friend to share their thoughts, but it does not convey that you understand much at all. This question is pretty useful, but it does not guess at unstated feelings at all.

A more closed-ended question shows understanding, but does not leave much room for them to correct you. For example the closed-ended question "did that make you feel upset?"" suggests the person should answer yes or no. It does not explicitly invite them to elaborate. They may feel pressured to answer yes or no, even if neither is a satisfying answer for them. If your guess is close but not quite accurate, yes and no could both be bad answers. Thankfully, we have a spectrum of options to choose from. The options in the middle of the spectrum are often my favorite ones. Here are several examples, from the most open-ended at the top to the most closed-ended at the bottom:

1. "How did that make you feel?" (no guesses at all)
2. "How did that make you feel? Upset?" (open-ended, with a guess)

3. "Did that make you feel confused, or upset, or frustrated?" (several guesses, leaving room for nuance)
4. "Did that make you feel upset?" (if they answer yes or no then there is not room for nuance)
5. "Oh, so you felt sad." (this is not even a question; it invites no nuance)

I tend to lean on questions like the second and third ones from this list. These ones in the middle of the spectrum strike a balance between conveying understanding and leaving room for correction.

Confidence Level Spectrum

The second tool is the confidence level spectrum. Here I am not talking about your confidence as a person, but rather how you can explicitly indicate your confidence level in each statement you make, like the "I'm sure" in "I'm sure you felt upset". This confidence level spectrum is for explicitly indicating confidence level in your guesses.

When you are confident you understand your friend, conveying that confidence can be pretty validating! When you are less confident or unsure, it is more important to leave room for correction. You do not want to accidentally invalidate them. You may be surprised at how much nuance people add when they are given space to share! Here are some examples on the confidence-level spectrum, from more confident at the top to less confident at the bottom:

1. "I'm sure you were thrilled to hear that!" (expressing certainty with "I'm sure")
2. "You must have felt really isolated, huh." (a confident guess)
3. "I imagine maybe you had mixed feelings about that,

happy and sad both?" (not sure, just imagining)
4. "I don't think I have this quite right... when you heard X you felt Y?" (trying to guess, very low confidence)
5. "I can't imagine what you must have been feeling. What was it like?" (totally not sure)

On this confidence level spectrum, just as with the open-closed spectrum, I tend to use the middle more than the extremes. I do sometimes use items from the full range of both of these, too. It's contextual! These are two tools you can use to help you more deliberately choose how to support your friend. These are not strict guidelines.

What else can help you be sure your friend is comfortable correcting you? You can phrase your guesses carefully, but comfort level also varies person to person, and also relationship to relationship. Some people are just inherently more comfortable correcting others, and that can be one big factor. Your relationship with the person may be even more important; when they trust that you are earnestly trying to understand them, they may be more willing to correct your guesses. If for any reason your friend is not comfortable correcting your guesses, you may want to lean on other validation techniques instead.

4 - Validate Based on the Past

In this next level of validation, you communicate to your friend that their response makes sense given their past experiences. For example, most people are not afraid of using kitchen knives but you may know at least one person who is. Perhaps they have been cut by a kitchen knife while chopping vegetables, or perhaps they have seen someone else get cut. If they have had any experience like this before then it would totally make sense that this fear might still be with them today.

For validation purposes, it does not matter if they *could* overcome this fear. If their fear can make sense based on their past, focusing on that past experience can be validating. It is validating to affirm that their current experience makes sense, and it is validating to affirm that their past makes sense as a factor.

5 - Validate Based on Today

In level five, you communicate that their response makes sense for anyone in the current situation. Their response makes sense regardless of their past, since anybody could be expected to have that response.

For example, imaging your friend is afraid of holding a snake. Since most people are afraid of snakes, it makes sense your friend would be too — that acknowledgment can be pretty deeply validating. Some research even suggests that human brains are wired to be afraid of certain things more than others, including snakes and spiders[17].

In this level it does not even matter so much whether they were bit by a snake as a child or not. People are inherently afraid of snakes. It is usually more validating to focus on "anybody would feel this" rather than "oh it makes sense for *you*, based on your past". I find myself leaning on this fifth level of validation "validate based on

[17]Martin E. P. Seligman, "Phobias and Preparedness," *Behavior Therapy* 2, no. 3 (July 1971): 307–20, https://doi.org/10.1016/S0005-7894(71)80064-3.

today" more than I lean on the fourth level "validate based on the past."

6 - Radical Genuineness

For some experiences, you might relate very deeply yourself. Sharing a very similar experience can be the most validating thing of all. For example, imagine you are supporting a friend whose grandmother just passed away, and your grandmother also passed away recently. Sharing your experience and how it made you feel can be very validating.

Be careful with this level - it is only achievable if the other person believes the experience is truly similar. For example, imagine a friend whose child has passed away recently. If you were to assert strongly that you deeply relate to a friend's child passing away because you lost your father, that could be in fact quite invalidating. Losing a child is such a uniquely terrible experience that there are support groups explicitly dedicated to parents who have lost children. It is great that you are trying to relate, but only the other person can determine how much your experience feels relevant. It is often much more effective to listen to the other person's experience. To ignore the nuance of the other person's situation, even accidentally, is a recipe for invalidation.

All that being said, if your experience does feel very relevant to them, that can be *deeply* validating. It can be very powerful to know that another person has experienced something so similar to you. When validation happens at this sixth level of validation, it can be more validating than any of the other levels.

Asking Too Much?

Sharing your emotions with others can be really beneficial for your relationship. It can make you feel understood and bring you both closer together.

However, asking for too much emotional support could be an issue. If you expect your friend to do more *emotional labor* for you than they are comfortable doing, they may resent it. In an imbalanced relationship, one side supports the other disproportionately. There may be an imbalance in how much emotional support you each have available to provide, or in how much emotional support you each need. The important part is that you communicate about it. Set healthy boundaries with your close friends by prioritizing communicating these concerns. Communicate about how you like to give and receive support.

A friend's support can go a long way, but for deeper issues or trauma, friends alone may not be enough. Think about whether your friend's support is enough, or if a professional therapist might help more. If you have not tried therapy before, you should consider at least letting them do a screening test to see if you would benefit from it.

Suggested Activities

1. Read more about the Six Levels of Validation
    - For another high level summary, read the article "Understanding Validation: A Way to Communicate Acceptance" by Karyn Hall[18].

[18]Karyn Hall, "Understanding Validation: A Way to Communicate

- For a deeper dive, read the original source "Validation and Psychotherapy" by Marsha Linehan[19].

2. Ask a friend if they want to talk about something that has been bothering them. Try multiple levels of validation, and pay attention to how they each resonate differently.

Acceptance," *Psychology Today*, April 26, 2012, https://www.psychologytoday.com/us/blog/pieces-mind/201204/understanding-validation-way-communicate-acceptance.

[19] Marsha M. Linehan, "Validation and Psychotherapy." in *Empathy Reconsidered: New Directions in Psychotherapy.*, ed. Arthur C. Bohart and Leslie S. Greenberg (Washington: American Psychological Association, 1997), 353–92, https://doi.org/10.1037/10226-016.

Cognitive Restructuring

You have learned a lot so far, including: how to enter an introspective state, how to take stock of the inputs to your system, how to process experiences by putting them into words, and how to validate those experiences. In this chapter, you will learn how to identify and counter unhelpful thought patterns, turning them into helpful ones. This is known as *cognitive restructuring*.

Cognitive Restructuring is the process of identifying and countering *maladaptive thought patterns*. Maladaptive means "unhelpful" or "counterproductive." Maladaptive thought patterns are ones that do a bad job of being helpful ("mal" meaning bad, and "adaptive" meaning helpful). A more colloquial synonym for this is *unhelpful thought patterns*. Unchecked, these thought patterns can lead to downward spirals of negative emotion, making you feel worse in an unproductive, unhelpful way.

The rest of this chapter focuses on a specific type of maladaptive thought pattern: *cognitive distortions*. A cognitive distortion gives you a skewed, inaccurate view of reality. They tend to be irrational or exaggerated. First we will cover the common cognitive distortions, and then go through an example scenario where we identify and counter those cognitive distortions we encounter.

Common Cognitive Distortions

Once you can identify that a thought contains a cognitive distortion, you can begin to counter it. You can get pretty far even just being able to think to yourself "I can feel it, this thought contains a cognitive distortion". To go a step further, it can help to know which cognitive distortions apply. A thought can contain multiple cognitive distortions.

Knowing the name(s) of which cognitive distortions apply can help you put into words how it is one. It can give you more confidence, and help you focus on how to counter it. Using their names can also help you communicate about them with other people.

Here we cover eleven of the most common cognitive distortions. They are presented in five groups of two or three distortions each to make them easier to remember. Many of these thought patterns could fit in multiple of the groups. These eleven most common cognitive distortions in five groups are:

1. Facts or Feelings
    - emotional reasoning
    - post-hoc rationalization
2. Needs Nuance
    - overgeneralization
    - labeling

    - all-or-nothing thinking
3. Positives and Negatives
    - magnification and minimization
    - disqualifying the positive
4. People
    - personalization
    - mind reading
5. Outcome Prediction
    - fortune-telling
    - catastrophization

Facts or Feelings

- **Emotional Reasoning** is when you believe something based on a feeling, as opposed to thinking about it and basing it on facts.
- **Post-hoc Rationalization** is when you have already made up your mind based on a gut feeling and you defend that gut feeling with facts you come up with afterward. "Post-hoc" meaning "after the event."

Needs Nuance

- **Overgeneralization** is applying a small amount of information to explain a whole situation, inaccurately. It is when you do not incorporate enough nuance.
- **Labeling** is a subset of overgeneralization. This is using a short-hand description which leaves a lot implied. This misses a lot of what makes the person or situation unique.
- **All-or-nothing thinking** is when you think in a binary yes/no or good/bad kind of way. Truth often lies in a gray area between the two extremes.

Positives and Negatives

- **Magnification** is focusing too much on something (often negative), and **minimization** is focusing too little on something (often positive).
- **Disqualifying the positive** is when you convince yourself that certain positive things do not count. This could be completely discounting the positive or partially discounting it, reducing the relative weight of importance you give it.

People

- **Personalization** is believing you have more control or influence over a situation than you actually do. This often happens when you focus on ways you yourself could have affected the situation, and you do not take in to account forces external to yourself.
- **Mind reading** is believing you know what another person is thinking or feeling without any evidence.

Outcome Prediction

- **Fortune-telling** is believing you know how something will turn out, usually for the worse.
- **Catastrophization** is focusing on the worst possible outcome of a situation, especially when it is a less likely outcome.

You can learn even more of these by searching online for "cognitive distortions" or "maladaptive thought patterns." One place to start is the Wikipedia article on cognitive distortions[20]. This Wikipedia article is particularly easy to

[20] https://en.wikipedia.org/wiki/Cognitive_distortion

find when you need it. If you want to share the concept of cognitive distortions with anyone else, this article covers the basic idea well enough, too.

Example Scenario

One evening I was excited to attend a tech event. I was wet and cold from being in the rain. On my way to the event I even stepped in a puddle! I heard several thoughts go off in my head. These thoughts made me feel worse, and I really considered not going. I gave myself a "whoop!" to introspect a bit, and took stock of my automatic thoughts, including:

- "Ugh! Wet shoes are the worst!"
- "If I'm running late, I shouldn't even go!"
- "Today sucks."

Which cognitive distortions apply to these automatic thoughts?

My first thought "wet shoes are the worst" is an example of **magnification**. It blows the problem out of proportion — not only are wet shoes bad, but they are magnified to be the WORST. This is also **emotional reasoning** since I am coming up with this based on my mood, and not based on facts. I would not consider this **post hoc rationalization** since I am not defending this thought with any support.

My second thought "If I'm running late, I just shouldn't go!" is an example of **all or nothing thinking**. By this perspective, one option is arriving on time, and another option is not going at all, but anything between is not an option. Digging deeper, the implied reason in my mind is "because arriving late will look bad." That reasoning is an example of **mind reading** and **fortune telling** that when I arrive late, the folks at the event would judge me. This is also potentially **disqualifying the positive** things that would make attending worthwhile, like learning and making connections with people.

My third thought "today sucks" has a lot going on. This is an example of **overgeneralizing** the entire day, **disqualifying the positive** things that happened earlier in the day, and **fortune telling** that the rest of the day is also going to be bad.

Once you identify which cognitive distortions you are experiencing, take a moment to be proud. It is challenging to learn this skill of identifying cognitive distortions! Even if you don't know what to do with them next, celebrate their identification. Celebrate that you took a moment to be introspective. Celebrate that you took stock of automatic thoughts and feelings, and that you are working on debugging your brain.

The Three Column Technique

Once you know which cognitive distortions you are experiencing, you can address them one at a time. The "three column technique" can help with this (adapted from "Feeling Good: The New Mood Therapy"[21]).

The left column is for describing your unhelpful *automatic thoughts*. The middle column is for identifying which cognitive distortions apply to those thoughts, like we did for the examples just now. The right column is for writing out more adaptive, deliberate thoughts to counter the

[21] Burns, *Feeling Good*.

automatic thoughts.

In the examples above we were focusing on the the first two columns: automatic thoughts and cognitive distortions. We listed several cognitive distortions for each automatic thought. We focused on describing the current situation in those. In the third column we focus on what we can do next.

Three Column Technique

Automatic Thought	Cognitive Distortions	More Adaptive Thought
"wet shoes are the worst"	**magnification**, emotional reasoning	
"if I'm running late, I just shouldn't go"	**all or nothing thinking**, mind reading, fortune telling, disqualifying the positive	
"today sucks"	**disqualifying the positive**, overgeneralizing, fortune telling	

Figure 9: The Three Column Technique table with columns one and two completed, but column three left blank.

Our next step is to counter those maladaptive automatic thoughts with more adaptive alternatives. When countering cognitive distortions, I like to focus on one at a time.

My first thought "wet shoes are the worst" contains the cognitive distortion **magnification**. I can adjust this thought to be more accurate and rational by thinking something, like "Wet shoes are not literally the worst, obviously. I am feeling really uncomfortable and cold right now, and these wet shoes are making it worse. It's really unfortunate this happened." This may not be as satisfying to exclaim as "wet shoes are the worst!," but that is the point — this defuses you, and prevents you from experiencing a downward spiral of even more negative automatic thoughts and emotions.

My second thought "If I'm running late, I just shouldn't go!" contains the distortion **all or nothing thinking**. I could defuse this with something like "The gray area answer is often pretty good, let's think about it more. I thought going was worth it before, and it's probably still pretty worthwhile. Is it really that bad to be late? Will it make me look so bad that it's literally not worth attending? No! Actually yeah, the topic is great and the people are great and I think I'll enjoy going."

My third thought "today sucks" contains the distortion **disqualifying the positive** things that happened earlier in the day and what could still happen. To counter this I might try and come up with a couple of positive things that happened that day like "well, brunch this morning was good at least." I might also think about the positives of being able to attend a meetup at all, like "I'm glad I have the free time and energy to attend meetups lately, even wet. Not everyone has this opportunity."

With these more adaptive counter-thoughts written out in the third column, the three column technique is complete!

While you are learning this technique it can be helpful

Three Column Technique

Automatic Thought	Cognitive Distortions	More Adaptive Thought
"wet shoes are the worst"	**magnification**, emotional reasoning	"I am uncomfortable and cold, and that is unfortunate"
"if I'm running late, I just shouldn't go"	**all or nothing thinking**, mind reading, fortune telling, disqualifying the positive	"going late is still valuable, and it won't actually look that bad"
"today sucks"	**disqualifying the positive**, overgeneralizing, fortune telling	"I'm glad I get to go to a meetup at all"

Figure 10: The Three Column Technique table with all three columns completed.

to write out the full chart. You may be surprised how different it is to write it out versus just thinking it. Once you develop this skill you may be able to imagine this chart in your head more effectively. Even then, you may still want to write it out more fully for any particularly challenging or new experiences.

Suggested Activity

Try the three column technique yourself! Get out a piece of paper or pull up something on your computer to write on. Think about a time recently when you were very frustrated about something, a time when you experienced a downward spiral. In the left column, write out some automatic thoughts. In the middle column, write out any cognitive distortions that apply. Feel free to reference the list of them earlier in this chapter. These first two columns are descriptive of what is happening. In the right column, write out any alternative more-adaptive thoughts you can think of.

Key Takeaways

We have covered many concepts in a short space in this book. Let's do a quick recap of the main ideas, from the top.

A **downward spiral** is a counterproductive feedback loop. It stems from negative thoughts leading to negative feelings leading to more negative thoughts. Downward spirals can be exacerbated by **cognitive distortions**. To deal with these cognitive distortions, it helps to identify and counter them. **Cognitive Behavioral "Training"** is a common and effective approach to dealing with cognitive distortions.

We worked with a simple model of the brain, using the **input-process-output model**. When a person is being mindful they are able to influence the process part of their mind. When on autopilot, they cannot. Looking at the **Inner versus Outer brain dichotomy**, we saw that emotions often happen faster than thoughts. Both thoughts and emotions are important to be aware of when debugging.

To begin debugging your brain you must first enter a mindful, **introspective state**. You can enter this introspective state either during an experience, or afterwards. One way to enter this is by using **the whoop technique**. Once in this introspective state, you can notice inputs that are already outside of your control.

Automatic inputs to the conscious part of your mind include:

1. automatic thoughts
2. automatic feelings
3. external stimuli
4. bodily state.

From here, you can focus on what **deliberate thoughts** you choose to think. Through those deliberate thoughts you can influence your feelings, and choose a better outcome for the situation.

For processing experiences, we covered three principles: 1. verbalize experiences 2. avoid ruminating on experiences 3. accept your automatic inputs non-judgmentally as data

For processing experiences, we also covered six techniques, including:

1. talking with a friend
2. talking with a rubber duck
3. writing
4. meditating
5. reading fiction
6. expanding your emotional vocabulary

When you are supporting a friend and you want them to feel understood, try to explicitly validate them. There are **six levels of validation** you can leverage, including:

1. being present
2. accurately reflecting
3. carefully guessing at unstated feelings
4. validating based on their past
5. validating based on today
6. radical genuineness.

You can use the **three column technique** to help analyze your thought patterns for cognitive distortions. Identify the **automatic thoughts**, identify the **cognitive distortions** in those, and the think of **more adaptive counter-thoughts**. The eleven most common cognitive distortions in five groups are:

1. Facts or Feelings
    - emotional reasoning
    - post-hoc rationalization
2. Needs Nuance
    - overgeneralization
    - labeling
    - all-or-nothing thinking
3. Positives and Negatives
    - magnification and minimization
    - disqualifying the positive
4. People
    - personalization
    - mind reading
5. Outcome Prediction
    - fortune-telling
    - catastrophization

Whew, we have covered a lot! To internalize the skills covered in this book, you will need to practice them. The next time you find yourself in a difficult situation or downward spiraling, try to remember the relevant parts of this book. Feel free to come back to this book to jog your memory. Many people regularly revisit Debugging Your Brain, and each time they get new insights. By practicing these skills you, too, will become a skilled debugger of your brain.

More Resources

Bibliotherapy

Bibliotherapy is therapy via reading, as opposed to talking with a therapist. Reading certain books has been shown to be as effective as in-person therapy for some people[22]. It is also much less expensive than therapy, too. The more motivated you are, the more likely bibliotherapy is to help. If you can also see a therapist regularly, that combination is the best option for working on these skills. Your therapist may even ask you to read a book as homework.

In particular, I recommend the book that popularized CBT, "Feeling Good: The New Mood Therapy" by David Burns. This book covers cognitive distortions very in-depth, with many vivid examples. This book is intended for you to use at home, even without a therapist. Many of my friends have read this book, and they rave about it. It has changed their lives for the better.

---

[22]Gualano et al., "The Long-Term Effects of Bibliotherapy in Depression Treatment."

Talk Therapy

Talk therapy with a therapist is often the very best way to get better at debugging your brain. A therapist will determine how they can best help you, whether they make a formal diagnosis or not. If you think of Cognitive Behavioral Therapy as "training," therapists happen to be skilled personal trainers.

Two of the most frequent diagnoses are depression and anxiety. Unfortunately, many folks who have these have not been diagnosed yet. Even mild depression and mild anxiety, can still affect your life in very significant ways. These two mental issues in particular can benefit from the skills you would develop through therapy.

A good place to start is through your health insurance plan, see which therapists are covered. If you can see one of these it may be the most cost effective approach. If you cannot find one through your health insurance, there are other options available too. Many places offer a sliding scale based on income. There may be other assistance programs available in your area, too. If you believe therapy would help you, there is probably a way to get it.

Teletherapy

There are some remote "teletherapy" options you may consider as well. These are not quite the same as traditional in-office talk therapy, but they can be more affordable and scheduling can be more flexible. For examples, two teletherapy companies that are popular lately are Talkspace and Better Help.

Apps

The web application Joyable helps with one particular issue, social anxiety. It is a great tool to help make sure you regularly work on your CBT homework, and give you some structure around it. It is cheaper than seeing a therapist, but just as with the book approach seeing a therapist in conjunction with the app is more effective.

Joyable is a great tool for social anxiety. I have not yet found an app that helps with CBT more generally, but I really hope to see more things like this!

Meditation

Meditation has a lot of health benefits. There are many studies showing that it decreases stress, anxiety, and depression. Some doctors even "prescribe" meditation to their patients.

There are many ways to get started with meditation — apps, videos, books, classes. I suggest trying out the apps "Headspace" and/or "Calm" for an introduction, they are each very approachable for people new to meditation.

Regular Practice

Regardless of your approach, you will have to regularly practice these skills to see progress. Brainstorm about how you will get yourself to regularly work on these skills. You might come up with some prompts like calendar event reminders, or practicing immediately before or after doing something else. You might pick one maladaptive thought pattern per week to look out for and work on, or you might set a goal of *whooping* yourself once per day. There are entire books on the psychology of habit formation you could dig into. However you are able, make debugging your brain a habit for yourself.

References

Bal, P. Matthijs, and Martijn Veltkamp. "How Does Fiction Reading Influence Empathy? An Experimental Investigation on the Role of Emotional Transportation." *PloS One* 8, no. 1 (2013): e55341. https://doi.org/10.1371/journal.pone.0055341.

Burns, David D. *Feeling Good: The New Mood Therapy*. Rev. and updated. New York: Avon, 1999.

Gualano, M. R., F. Bert, M. Martorana, G. Voglino, V. Andriolo, R. Thomas, C. Gramaglia, P. Zeppegno, and R. Siliquini. "The Long-Term Effects of Bibliotherapy in Depression Treatment: Systematic Review of Randomized Clinical Trials." *Clinical Psychology Review* 58 (December 2017): 49–58. https://doi.org/10.1016/j.cpr.2017.09.006.

Hall, Karyn. "Understanding Validation: A Way to Communicate Acceptance." *Psychology Today*, April 26, 2012. https://www.psychologytoday.com/us/blog/pieces-mind/201204/understanding-validation-way-communicate-acceptance.

Hofmann, Stefan G., Anu Asnaani, Imke J. J. Vonk, Alice T. Sawyer, and Angela Fang. "The Efficacy of Cognitive Behavioral Therapy: A Review of Meta-Analyses." *Cognitive Therapy and Research* 36, no. 5 (October 1, 2012): 427–40. https://doi.org/10.1007/s10608-012-9476-1.

Kahneman, Daniel. *Thinking, Fast and Slow*. 1st pbk. ed. New York: Farrar, Straus and Giroux, 2013.

King, Marissa. "Working to Address the Loneliness Epidemic: Perspective-Taking, Presence, and Self-Disclosure." *American Journal of Health Promotion* 32, no. 5 (June 2018): 1315–7. https://doi.org/10.1177/0890117118776735c.

Linehan, Marsha M. "Validation and Psychotherapy." In *Empathy Reconsidered: New Directions in Psychotherapy.*, edited by Arthur C. Bohart and Leslie S. Greenberg, 353–92. Washington: American Psychological Association, 1997. https://doi.org/10.1037/10226-016.

Maddox, Stephanie A., Casey S. Watts, Valérie Doyère, and Glenn E. Schafe. "A Naturally-Occurring Histone Acetyltransferase Inhibitor Derived from Garcinia Indica Impairs Newly Acquired and Reactivated Fear Memories." *PloS One* 8, no. 1 (2013): e54463. https://doi.org/10.1371/journal.pone.0054463.

Maddox, Stephanie A., Casey S. Watts, and Glenn E. Schafe. "DNA Methyltransferase Activity Is Required for Memory-Related Neural Plasticity in the Lateral Amygdala." *Neurobiology of Learning and Memory* 107 (January 2014): 93–100. https://doi.org/10.1016/j.nlm.2013.11.008.

———. "P300/CBP Histone Acetyltransferase Activity Is Required for Newly Acquired and Reactivated Fear Memories in the Lateral Amygdala." *Learning & Memory (Cold Spring Harbor, N.Y.)* 20, no. 2 (January 17, 2013): 109–19. https://doi.org/10.1101/lm.029157.112.

Polack, Ellie. "New Cigna Study Reveals Loneliness at Epidemic Levels in America." Cigna, a Global Health Insurance and Health Service Company. Accessed July 19, 2020. https://www.cigna.com/newsroom/news-releases/2018/new-cigna-study-reveals-loneliness-at-epidemic-levels-in-america.

Seligman, Martin E. P. "Phobias and Preparedness." *Behavior Therapy* 2, no. 3 (July 1971): 307–20. https://doi.org/10.1016/S0005-7894(71)80064-3.

Silverstein, David N., and Martin Ingvar. "A Multi-Pathway Hypothesis for Human Visual Fear Signaling." *Frontiers in Systems Neuroscience* 9 (2015): 101. https://doi.org/10.3389/fnsys.2015.00101.

Stanovich, Keith E., and Richard F. West. "Individual Differences in Reasoning: Implications for the Rationality Debate?" *Behavioral and Brain Sciences* October 2000, no. 23(5) (n.d.): 645–65.

Watts, Casey S. "Six Types of Hunger." Blog. Casey Watts Blog, December 18, 2017. https://caseywatts.com/2017/12/18/types-of-hunger.html.

Wells, Adrian, and Panagiotis Roussis. "Refraining from Intrusive Thoughts Is Strategy Dependent: A Comment on Sugiura, et Al. And a Preliminary Informal Test of Detached Mindfulness, Acceptance, and Other Strategies." *Psychological Reports* 115, no. 2 (October 2014):

541–44. https://doi.org/10.2466/02.PR0.115c21z9.

Zaidel, Dahlia W. "Split-Brain, the Right Hemisphere, and Art: Fact and Fiction." *Progress in Brain Research* 204 (2013): 3–17. https://doi.org/10.1016/B978-0-444-63287-6.00001-4.

CPSIA information can be obtained
at www.ICGtesting.com
Printed in the USA
LVHW052352151120
671610LV00006B/422

9 780578 755038